Slow Cooker MAGIC

Hearty Lentil Stew

1 cup dried lentils, rinsed and drained
1 package (16 ounces) frozen green beans
2 cups cauliflower florets
1 cup chopped onion
1 cup baby carrots, cut in half crosswise
3 cups fat-free reduced-sodium chicken broth
2 teaspoons ground cumin
¾ teaspoon ground ginger
1 can (15 ounces) chunky tomato sauce with garlic and herbs
½ cup dry-roasted peanuts

1. Place lentils in slow cooker. Top with green beans, cauliflower, onion and carrots. Combine broth, cumin and ginger in large bowl; mix well. Pour mixture over vegetables. Cover and cook on LOW 9 to 11 hours.

2. Stir in tomato sauce. Cover and cook on LOW 10 minutes. Ladle stew into bowls. Sprinkle peanuts evenly onto each serving.   *Makes 6 servings*

Hearty Lentil Stew

Vegetarian Chili

1 tablespoon vegetable oil
1 cup finely chopped onion
1 cup chopped red bell pepper
2 tablespoons minced jalapeño pepper*
1 clove garlic, minced
1 can (28 ounces) crushed tomatoes, undrained
1 can (14½ ounces) black beans, rinsed and drained
1 can (14 ounces) garbanzo beans, drained
½ cup canned corn
¼ cup tomato paste
1 teaspoon sugar
1 teaspoon ground cumin
1 teaspoon dried basil leaves
1 teaspoon chili powder
¼ teaspoon black pepper
1 cup shredded Cheddar cheese (optional)
Sour cream (optional)

*Jalapeño peppers can sting and irritate the skin; wear rubber gloves when handling peppers and do not touch eyes. Wash hands after handling.

1. Heat oil in large nonstick skillet over medium-high heat until hot. Add chopped onion, bell pepper, jalapeño pepper and garlic; cook and stir 5 minutes or until vegetables are tender.

2. Spoon vegetables into slow cooker. Add remaining ingredients, except cheese and sour cream; mix well. Cover and cook on LOW 4 to 5 hours. Garnish with cheese and sour cream, if desired.

Makes 4 servings

Vegetarian Chili

Middle Eastern Lamb Stew

1½ pounds lamb stew meat, cubed
2 tablespoons all-purpose flour
1 tablespoon vegetable oil
1½ cups beef broth
1 cup chopped onion
½ cup chopped carrots
1 clove garlic, minced
1 tablespoon tomato paste
½ teaspoon ground cumin
½ teaspoon red pepper flakes
¼ teaspoon ground cinnamon
½ cup chopped dried apricots
1 teaspoon salt
¼ teaspoon black pepper
3 cups hot cooked noodles

1. Coat lamb cubes with flour; set aside. Heat oil in large nonstick skillet over medium-high heat until hot. Brown half of lamb and transfer to slow cooker; repeat with remaining lamb. Add broth, onion, carrots, garlic, tomato paste, cumin, red pepper and cinnamon. Cover and cook on LOW 3 hours.

2. Stir in apricots, salt and pepper. Cover and cook on LOW 2 to 3 hours, or until lamb is tender and sauce is thickened. Serve lamb over noodles.

Makes 6 servings

Ham and Potato Casserole

1½ pounds red potatoes, peeled and sliced
8 ounces thinly sliced ham
2 poblano chili peppers, cut into thin strips
2 tablespoons olive oil
1 tablespoon dried oregano leaves
¼ teaspoon salt
1 cup (4 ounces) shredded Monterey Jack cheese
with or without hot peppers
2 tablespoons finely chopped cilantro leaves

1. Combine all ingredients, except cheese and cilantro, in slow cooker; mix well. Cover and cook on LOW 7 hours or on HIGH 4 hours.

2. Transfer potato mixture to serving dish and sprinkle with cheese and cilantro. Let stand 3 minutes or until cheese melts. *Makes 6 to 7 servings*

Parmesan Potato Wedges

2 pounds red potatoes, cut into ½-inch wedges
¼ cup finely chopped yellow onion
2 tablespoons butter, cut into ⅛-inch pieces
1½ teaspoons dried oregano leaves
½ teaspoon salt
Black pepper to taste
¼ cup (1 ounce) grated Parmesan cheese

Layer potatoes, onion, butter, oregano, salt and pepper in slow cooker. Cook on HIGH 4 hours. Transfer potatoes to serving platter and sprinkle with cheese.
Makes 6 servings

Sweet and Sour Spare Ribs

    4 pounds spare ribs
    2 cups dry sherry or chicken broth
    ½ cup pineapple, mango or guava juice
    ⅓ cup chicken broth
    1 clove garlic, minced
    2 tablespoons brown sugar
    2 tablespoons cider vinegar
    2 tablespoons soy sauce
    ½ teaspoon salt
    ¼ teaspoon black pepper
    ⅛ teaspoon red pepper flakes
    1 tablespoon cornstarch

1. Preheat oven to 400°F. Place ribs in foil-lined shallow roasting pan. Bake 30 minutes, turning over after 15 minutes. Remove from oven. Slice meat into 2-rib portions. Place ribs in 5-quart slow cooker. Add remaining ingredients, except cornstarch, to slow cooker.

2. Cover and cook on LOW 6 hours. Uncover and skim fat from liquid.

3. Combine cornstarch and ¼ cup liquid from slow cooker; stir until smooth. Pour mixture back into slow cooker; mix well. Cover and cook on HIGH 10 minutes or until slightly thickened.   *Makes 4 servings*

Sweet and Sour Spare Ribs

Shredded Pork Wraps

1 cup salsa, divided
2 tablespoons cornstarch
1 bone-in pork sirloin roast (2 pounds)
6 (8-inch) flour tortillas
⅓ cup shredded reduced-fat Cheddar cheese
3 cups broccoli slaw mix

1. Combine ¼ cup salsa and cornstarch in small bowl; stir until smooth. Pour mixture into slow cooker. Top with pork roast. Pour remaining ¾ cup salsa over roast.

2. Cover and cook on LOW 6 to 8 hours or until internal temperature reaches 165°F when tested with meat thermometer inserted into the thickest part of roast, not touching bone. Remove roast from slow cooker. Transfer roast to cutting board; cover with foil and let stand 10 to 15 minutes or until cool enough to handle before shredding. Internal temperature will rise 5° to 10°F during stand time. Trim and discard outer fat from pork. Using 2 forks, pull pork into coarse shreds.

3. Divide shredded meat evenly on each tortilla. Spoon about 2 tablespoons salsa mixture on top of meat in each tortilla. Top evenly with cheese and broccoli slaw mix. Fold bottom edge of tortilla over filling; fold in sides. Roll up completely to enclose filling. Repeat with remaining tortillas. Serve remaining salsa mixture as a dipping sauce. *Makes 6 servings*

Shredded Pork Wrap

Southwestern Turkey in Chilies and Cream

1 boneless skinless turkey breast, cut into 1-inch
    pieces
2 tablespoons plus 2 teaspoons flour, divided
1 can (15 ounces) corn, well-drained
1 can (4 ounces) diced green chilies, well-drained
1 tablespoon butter
½ cup chicken broth
1 clove garlic, minced
1 teaspoon salt
½ teaspoon paprika
¼ teaspoon dried oregano leaves
¼ teaspoon black pepper
½ cup heavy cream
2 tablespoons chopped cilantro
3 cups hot cooked rice or pasta

1. Coat turkey pieces with 2 tablespoons flour; set aside.
Place corn and green chilies in slow cooker.

2. Melt butter in large nonstick skillet over medium
heat. Add turkey pieces; cook and stir 5 minutes or until
lightly browned. Place turkey in slow cooker. Add broth,
garlic, salt, paprika, oregano and pepper. Cover and cook
on LOW 2 hours.

3. Stir cream and remaining 2 teaspoons flour in small
bowl until smooth. Pour mixture into slow cooker. Cover
and cook on HIGH 10 minutes or until slightly
thickened. Stir in cilantro. Serve over rice.

Makes 6 (1½ cup) servings

Country Captain Chicken

4 chicken thighs
2 tablespoons all-purpose flour
2 tablespoons vegetable oil, divided
1 cup chopped green bell pepper
1 large onion, chopped
1 celery stalk, chopped
1 clove garlic, minced
¼ cup chicken broth
2 cups canned or fresh crushed tomatoes
½ cup golden raisins
1½ teaspoons curry powder
1 teaspoon salt
¼ teaspoon paprika
¼ teaspoon black pepper
2 cups hot cooked rice

1. Coat chicken with flour; set aside. Heat 1 tablespoon oil in large skillet over medium-high heat until hot. Add bell pepper, onion, celery and garlic. Cook and stir 5 minutes or until vegetables are tender. Place vegetables in slow cooker.

2. Heat remaining tablespoon oil in same skillet over medium-high heat. Add chicken and cook 5 minutes per side. Place chicken in slow cooker.

3. Pour broth into skillet. Heat over medium-high heat, stirring frequently and scraping up any browned bits from bottom of skillet. Pour liquid into slow cooker. Add tomatoes, raisins, curry powder, salt, paprika and pepper. Cover and cook on LOW 3 hours. Serve chicken with sauce over rice. *Makes 4 servings*

Broccoli & Cheese Strata

2 cups chopped broccoli florets
4 slices firm white bread, ½-inch thick
4 teaspoons butter
1½ cups (6 ounces) shredded Cheddar cheese
3 eggs
1½ cups reduced-fat (2%) milk
½ teaspoon salt
½ teaspoon hot pepper sauce
⅛ teaspoon black pepper

1. Cook broccoli in boiling water 10 minutes or until tender. Drain. Spread one side of each bread slice with 1 teaspoon butter.

2. Arrange 2 slices bread, buttered sides up in greased 1-quart casserole. Layer cheese, broccoli and remaining 2 bread slices, buttered sides down.

3. Beat together eggs, milk, salt, hot pepper sauce and pepper in medium bowl. Gradually pour over bread.

4. Place small wire rack in 5-quart slow cooker. Pour in 1 cup water. Place casserole on rack. Cover and cook on HIGH 3 hours.   *Makes 4 servings*

Broccoli & Cheese Strata

Beef and Vegetables in
Rich Burgundy Sauce

1 package (8 ounces) sliced mushrooms
1 package (8 ounces) baby carrots
1 medium green bell pepper, cut into thin strips
1 boneless chuck roast (2½ pounds)
1 can (10½ ounces) golden mushroom soup,
   undiluted
¼ cup dry red wine or beef broth
1 tablespoon Worcestershire sauce
1 package (1 ounce) dried onion soup mix
¼ teaspoon black pepper
2 tablespoons water
3 tablespoons cornstarch
4 cups hot cooked noodles
   Chopped fresh parsley (optional)

1. Place mushrooms, carrots and bell pepper in slow cooker. Place roast on top of vegetables. Combine soup, wine, Worcestershire sauce, soup mix and black pepper in medium bowl; mix well. Pour soup mixture over roast. Cover and cook on LOW 8 to 10 hours.

2. Blend water into cornstarch in cup until smooth; set aside. Transfer roast to cutting board; cover with foil. Let stand 10 to 15 minutes before slicing.

3. Turn slow cooker to HIGH. Stir cornstarch mixture into vegetable mixture; cover and cook 10 minutes or until thickened. Serve over noodles. Garnish with parsley, if desired.   *Makes 6 to 8 servings*

*Beef and Vegetables in
Rich Burgundy Sauce*

Mu Shu Turkey

1 can (16 ounces) plums, drained, rinsed and pitted
½ cup orange juice
¼ cup finely chopped onion
1 tablespoon minced fresh ginger
¼ teaspoon ground cinnamon
1 pound boneless turkey breast, cut into thin strips
6 (7-inch) flour tortillas
3 cups coleslaw mix

1. Place plums in blender or food processor. Cover and blend until almost smooth. Combine plums, orange juice, onion, ginger and cinnamon in slow cooker; mix well. Place turkey strips over plum mixture. Cover and cook on LOW 3 to 4 hours.

2. Remove turkey strips from slow cooker and divide evenly among tortillas. Spoon about 2 tablespoons plum sauce over turkey. Top evenly with coleslaw mix. Fold bottom edge of tortilla over filling; fold in sides. Roll up to completely enclose filling. Repeat with remaining tortillas. Use remaining plum sauce for dipping.

Makes 6 servings

Mu Shu Turkey

Mediterranean Meatball Ratatouille

2 tablespoons olive oil, divided
1 pound mild Italian sausage, casings removed
1 package (8 ounces) sliced mushrooms
1 small eggplant, diced
1 zucchini, diced
½ cup chopped onion
1 clove garlic, minced
1 teaspoon dried oregano leaves, divided
1 teaspoon salt, divided
½ teaspoon black pepper, divided
1 tablespoon tomato paste
2 tomatoes, diced
2 tablespoons chopped fresh basil
1 teaspoon fresh lemon juice

1. Pour 1 tablespoon olive oil into 5-quart slow cooker. Shape sausage into 1-inch balls. Place half the meatballs in slow cooker. Add half the mushrooms, eggplant and zucchini. Add onion, garlic, ½ teaspoon oregano, ½ teaspoon salt and ¼ teaspoon pepper.

2. Add remaining meatballs, mushrooms, eggplant and zucchini. Add remaining oregano, salt and pepper. Top with remaining 1 tablespoon olive oil. Cover and cook on LOW 6 to 7 hours.

3. Stir in tomato paste and diced tomatoes. Cover and cook on LOW 15 minutes. Stir in basil and lemon juice; serve. *Makes 6 (1⅔ cup) servings*

Mediterranean Meatball Ratatouille

Swiss Cheese Scalloped Potatoes

2 pounds baking potatoes, peeled and thinly sliced
½ cup finely chopped yellow onion
¼ teaspoon salt
¼ teaspoon ground nutmeg
2 tablespoons butter, cut into ⅛-inch pieces
½ cup milk
2 tablespoons all-purpose flour
3 ounces Swiss cheese slices, torn into small pieces
¼ cup finely chopped green onions (optional)

1. Layer half the potatoes, ¼ cup onion, ⅛ teaspoon salt, ⅛ teaspoon nutmeg and 1 tablespoon butter in slow cooker. Repeat layers. Cover and cook on LOW 7 hours or on HIGH 4 hours. Remove potatoes with slotted spoon to serving dish.

2. Blend milk and flour in small bowl until smooth. Stir mixture into slow cooker. Add cheese; stir to combine. If slow cooker is on LOW, turn to HIGH, cover and cook until slightly thickened, about 10 minutes. Stir; pour cheese mixture over potatoes. Garnish with chopped green onions, if desired.   *Makes 5 to 6 servings*

*Swiss Cheese
Scalloped Potatoes*

Luscious Pecan Bread Pudding

    3 cups French bread cubes
    3 tablespoons chopped pecans, toasted
2¼ cups low-fat milk
    2 eggs, beaten
    ½ cup sugar
    1 teaspoon vanilla
    ¾ teaspoon ground cinnamon, divided
    ¾ cup reduced-calorie cranberry juice cocktail
1½ cups frozen pitted tart cherries
    2 tablespoons sugar substitute

1. Toss bread cubes and pecans in soufflé dish. Combine milk, eggs, sugar, vanilla and ½ teaspoon cinnamon in large bowl. Pour over bread mixture in soufflé dish. Cover tightly with foil. Make foil handles (see tip). Place soufflé dish in slow cooker. Pour hot water into slow cooker to come about 1½ inches from top of soufflé dish. Cover and cook on LOW 2 to 3 hours.

2. Meanwhile, stir together cranberry juice and remaining ¼ teaspoon cinnamon in small saucepan; stir in frozen cherries. Bring sauce to boil over medium heat, about 5 minutes. Remove from heat. Stir in sugar substitute.

3. Lift dish from slow cooker with foil handles. Serve with cherry sauce.   *Makes 6 servings*

Tip: To make foil handles, tear off three 18×2-inch strips of heavy foil or use regular foil folded to double thickness. Crisscross foil strips in spoke design and place in slow cooker to allow for easy removal of pudding.

*Luscious Pecan
Bread Pudding*

Chocolate Croissant Pudding

1½ cups milk

3 eggs

½ cup sugar

¼ cup unsweetened cocoa powder

½ teaspoon vanilla

¼ teaspoon salt

2 plain croissants, cut into 1-inch pieces

½ cup chocolate chips

¾ cup whipped cream (optional)

1. Beat milk, eggs, sugar, cocoa, vanilla and salt in medium bowl.

2. Grease 1-quart casserole. Layer half croissant pieces, chocolate chips and half egg mixture in casserole. Repeat layers with remaining croissant pieces and egg mixture.

3. Place small wire rack into 5-quart slow cooker and pour in 1 cup water. Place casserole on rack. Cover and cook on LOW 3 to 4 hours. Remove casserole from slow cooker. Top each serving with 2 tablespoons whipped cream, if desired. *Makes 6 servings*

Chocolate Croissant Pudding

Curried Snack Mix

3 tablespoons butter
2 tablespoons brown sugar
1½ teaspoons hot curry powder
¼ teaspoon salt
¼ teaspoon ground cumin
2 cups rice squares cereal
1 cup walnut halves
1 cup dried cranberries

Melt butter in large skillet. Add brown sugar, curry powder, salt and cumin; mix well. Add cereal, walnuts and cranberries; stir to coat. Spoon mixture into slow cooker. Cover and cook on LOW 3 hours. Remove cover; cook an additional 30 minutes.

Makes 16 servings

Cherry Rice Pudding

1½ cups milk
1 cup hot cooked rice
3 eggs, beaten
½ cup sugar
¼ cup dried cherries or cranberries
½ teaspoon almond extract
¼ teaspoon salt

Combine all ingredients in large bowl. Pour mixture into greased 1½-quart casserole. Cover with foil. Place small wire rack into 5-quart slow cooker and pour in 1 cup water. Place casserole on rack. Cover and cook on LOW 4 to 5 hours. Remove casserole from slow cooker. Let stand 15 minutes before serving.   *Makes 6 servings*